The Goddess Potential

The Goddess Potential

A Guide To Developing A Relationship With Your Inner Self

Allyson Leak & Tara Wallace

Goddess House Press, 2015

Cover illustration & design: Kia Kelliebrew

ISBN: 0692624961
ISBN 13: 9780692624968

Printed in the United States of America

THE GODDESS PRINCIPLES

CONTENTS

FOREWORD

I'm a student of life and believe in experience being life's best teacher; still I rely on 'study guides,' or directional moments to keep me moving in the right direction.

The Goddess Potential is one such book. Whether you're starting over, need a life reset, or just want to begin embracing you day to day, this book is essential to the way forward.

Self-love and self-mastery is a lifelong process, and during this process you will need to retrain yourself towards a more nurturing and self-affirming way of living. This book is a perfect tool for women trying to find and keep themselves. I was honored when Ally called and asked me to write the foreword and I hope you find it as inspiring as I have.

~Estelle Swaray

PREFACE

I have always been passionate about helping others—it is just a natural part of who I am. In college I was the co-founder of a women's empowerment magazine called *SHE* Magazine. After college, I started a women's empowerment blog with a goal to uplift women with positive interviews, articles, and tips. I always wanted to take many of the concepts that have worked in my growth and share them with others. In 2010 I started working on a book of affirmations. In 2014 I decided I wanted to keep the basic concept but write a whole new book from scratch and that's when I met Tara. I found Tara to be super sweet, down to earth, and extremely humble. She was also on a life mission towards empowering herself. We decided to write *The Goddess Potential.*

~Ally

ACKNOWLEDGEMENTS

I would like to first thank God…the ultimate Creator. You saved me at a very low time in my life years ago. Our relationship has helped me grow, mature, and understand the world from a more balanced perspective…You are awesome!

I want to thank my husband Elvis. You are my best friend, my soul mate, my rock, and the best father on the planet to our twin boys. I will love you forever.

I want to thank my twin boys Kian and Kai. You are what pure love looks like. My sweet boys, you are the best gift I've ever received and you inspire me to be a better person every single day.

I want to thank Shari Gilmore and Linda Leak-Ransom for help with editing this book. You were both thorough and encouraging and I appreciate you.

Last but not least, I would like to express my gratitude to my mom, family, and close friends who are dear to my heart and who saw me through this book, provided support, talked things over, read and offered comments—you are forever appreciated.

~*Ally*

I would like to thank my creator for my mind and body for giving me the ability to accomplish all that I have set out to, and for giving me the ability to know that everything is possible because you created everything.

To my children Jamison and Kaz thank you, for you are the ones that I owe my greatest self to as an example. I am your rock. I live so much for you boys and my life is so rich and fulfilled because of you.

To my mom, dad, siblings, and grandfather, the core of who I am comes from what we were growing up and the foundation that we built. Thank you for my strength and always believing that my strength would allow me to get through anything. It is that force that I live by.

And to friends and people that have taught me valuable life lessons, your words of wisdom have encouraged me and it feels great to know that you have been in my corner as a supporter of all things that make me better.
~Tara

INTRODUCTION

When a woman starts on a journey to better her inner self, it not only helps her but it can also create more unity and compassion throughout the world. While that sounds awesome in theory, life doesn't always make the journey to self-discovery easy. Every woman has the potential inside to shine bright and to achieve greatness. However, sometimes fear, painful pasts, and toxic environments hold her back. There is no magic secret to success, love, and happiness, but there are steps we can all take to help ourselves stay balanced and sane through all of life's ups and downs. What is the answer to keeping it all balanced? It is the bond with the inner self. And to get that, we must all unleash our own Goddess Potential.

The Goddess Potential uses eight principles with steps that will help you explore and embrace your inner self. Each principle begins with an affirmation read in the mirror. Why mirror affirmations? Because, retraining the brain combined with nurturing the spirit is the key to success. When you affirm the life you want by staring directly into your own eyes, it's almost like pressing the reset button in your brain. Plus, when information enters the brain through vision and hearing at the same time, it has a greater impact on memory and on storing the information.

Self-love and self-mastery is a lifelong journey and *The Goddess Potential* hopes to help you start that journey. Filled with inspirational steps, personal stories of success and failure, and a unique perspective on basic life principles, it is the perfect guide for women who are truly trying to find themselves. No matter where life has taken you, *The Goddess Potential* is a reminder that every day is an opportunity for a fresh start.

When you unleash your Goddess Potential, you will:

- Boost your self-esteem
- Worry less about what people think

- Have the confidence to reach for your dreams
- Have the courage to follow your instincts when it comes to love
- Be able to relax even in the presence of uncertainty
- Fall in love with your true self
- Support and not tear down other women

This book will work best read in stages. Once you complete the suggested tasks in each principle, then you should move on to the next principle. If you think it may be helpful, use a buddy system with a close friend to help you stay accountable. If you are interested in being a part of the #GoddessPotential community, which unifies, empowers, and connects you with other like-minded women, visit thegoddesspotential.com.

THE COURTSHIP-A DATE WITH SELF

If you were to look in the mirror and ask, "Who am I?" would you have an answer? Some people define themselves by their romantic relationships, jobs, social status, or in some other way that is totally outside of themselves. But what happens when those outside things we identify ourselves with go away? It can leave some people feeling lost, not knowing who they are or where they are going. And that's why the most important relationship any of us can possibly have is with the inner self because your inner self never goes anywhere—it is always with you. Plus, if you have a good foundation with your inner self, then it may help you withstand life's obstacles a little better. You can't be in a committed relationship with anyone until you are in a committed relationship with yourself. You may be used to someone courting you when they are dating you and now you are going to do that same thing. What does a healthy relationship with your inner self look like? It's honest, caring, loving, fun, and real. According to Dove Research "The Real Truth About Beauty: Revisited," eighty percent of women agree that every woman has something about her that is beautiful but do not see their own beauty.

AFFIRMATION

Look in the mirror and say:

"I am ready to fully unleash my Goddess Potential. I know I am a unique and special addition to this world. There is literally no one like me on the planet. I feel honored to be me."

Step 1-DON'T JUDGE YOURSELF TOO HARSHLY

Courting yourself starts with having less judgment. Ok, so in a perfect world, a little girl goes to grade school, finishes high school, goes to college or a trade school, starts a career, meets a great man, gets married and has five kids, right? Let's face it, we are brainwashed from youth to think that life is supposed to go in a certain order and when it doesn't (because it usually doesn't), we can feel like failures in society. Somehow these societal "norms" that are pushed on little girls and women have the ability to make some of us feel we are worthless unless we've achieved these milestones. There is no way that you are going to be able to release a lifetime of social judgment and brainwashing in the minute it takes you to read this paragraph. However, everything is about baby steps and it's important to remember that your life at this very moment is "ok." It's "ok" that you aren't married yet. It's "ok" that you haven't left the job you don't like yet. It's "ok" that you haven't checked off everything on your to-do list today or your to-do list for life. It's "ok" that the man in your life is not exactly who you want him to be. It's not that you have to be thrilled about all of your circumstances, but telling yourself it's "ok" means you aren't judging yourself too harshly for not fitting into what society says you should be. Think about it; every single decision you've ever made, whether it's what job to take, which route to drive when running errands, or which guy to date has all led to this moment, and they are all important in some way.

Step 2-REMEMBER THERE IS NO ONE ELSE LIKE YOU

When you court yourself, you should feel special and one way to do that is to remember that there is literally no one on the planet who is exactly like you. Regardless of your negative traits (everyone has them), remember you still bring a unique and special contribution to this planet just by being you. Remembering this comes in handy, especially when you may occasionally compare yourself to someone else.

Step 3-TAKE THE GODDESS INTERVIEW

Take a selfie with your phone because this picture and date represents the start of a new refreshed journey. Answer the following questions and write in pencil if possible:

Who are you?

_____

_____

_____

Who do you want to be?

_____

_____

_____

What do you love the most about your personality?

_____

_____

_____

What do you love the most about the way you look?

_____

_____

_____

Would you consider yourself as a glass half empty person or a glass half full person? Then, describe why.

_____

_____

_____

What do you desire?

_____

_____

_____

What brings you joy?

_____

_____

_____

What makes you laugh really hard?

_____

_____

_____

List ten goals for the next six months:

1. _____

2. _____

3. _____

4. _____

5. _____

6. _____

7. _____

8. _____

9. _____

10. _____

Now come back to this questionnaire in six months to see if any of your views have changed and how many of your goals you are actively working toward. Even if you have just started one or two things on your list, it's better than nothing, so still be proud of that.

Step 4-LEARN HOW TO SHUT IT ALL DOWN

There may come a time in your life where you find yourself just giving, giving and giving until you have nothing left to give. You could be helping a cousin with business advice, planning a baby shower for a friend, or doing favors for friends, family and neighbors all the time. Obviously you can't shut down your necessary obligations for your close family or kids, but there is always extra stuff you can shut down. Being selfish is necessary at times and not a bad thing when it comes to your peace of mind and courting yourself. How would you feel if a man you were dating was too busy to send a quick text or make a phone call? Think about it, the same way you would want him to make the relationship a priority; you also have to take the time and attention to conduct a courtship with yourself.

Step 5-PLAN A DATE NIGHT

Now that you have completed your first steps, the next step is a date with yourself. You are probably thinking, "I don't have the time." One way to avoid making excuses for your date night is to plan ahead. Let people know in advance that this date and this time you are not available. Whether you are just starting the journey to know the real you, or if you just need to get centered again in life, date night is the perfect way to do it. Pick a day where you don't have any responsibilities the following day, get good rest the night before and when you wake up in the morning let your instinct guide you to figure out what you should do. Do you want to start the day off with a cup of warm tea or treat yourself to breakfast? What about going for a walk in the park or reading a book there? You could also see if there are any cool workshops being offered in your area like painting, meditation, or dance. The whole point is for you to do whatever it is you want by yourself and to have a relaxing and stress free day doing exactly that.

Step 6-GIVE YOURSELF A SPONTANEOUS GIFT

So if you happen to be courted by a man that's really into you, he may show his love in various ways and sometimes that includes small thoughtful gifts. So why not give yourself those too? Pick up flowers for yourself or even a single rose once a month, buy a box of your favorite chocolates and wine or give yourself a spontaneous gift. And if your funds are low, write yourself a love letter or cook your favorite meal. The whole point is to get into a habit of just celebrating you for being you because you deserve it.

Step 7-KEEP A BUSY WOMAN'S JOURNAL

Who has time nowadays to write for hours upon hours in a journal each day? Whether it's running errands for kids, a demanding job, cooking for the family, or studying for a test in grad school, life can be super-busy. But just because life is busy doesn't mean there isn't a way to slow down for five minutes a day and write a few words or even just one word for reflection. A busy woman's journal has quick, short entries. If you had a great day and want to write pages about it, then fine. But if you don't have the time, it's entirely worthwhile to write one word and a smiley face. You could also buy a pack of stickers that have different emotions and just use the sticker to describe your day in a journal or on the calendar. That way, at least when you look back at it, you know you need to change something if the frowning stickers outnumber the happy ones. Creating a busy woman's journal is a great way to get your emotions and thoughts out for that day or week and then reflect and look back in six months from that date. By reflecting and looking back, you can see how much you've grown (or not grown) and what types of things you've accomplished. It just allows you to put things in perspective. And if you don't have a journal, you can use your phone or computer to make entries. Another creative idea related to the Busy Woman's Journal is to do a message in a jar. Buy a big jar and tiny rubber bands and leave a pen and small pad of paper next to it. Whenever you feel like it, write yourself a little note, put the date and roll it up to store in the jar. It can be anything you want. It could be a business idea, how you feel about your day, or an inspirational word. Whether your entry is daily, weekly or monthly, make sure you put in the date each time.

Step 8-LISTEN TO YOUR INSTINCT

When you court yourself, you become more in touch with your feelings and this awareness helps build your connection with your gut instinct. Most often we are taught to focus on "thinking things through," but we aren't taught how to listen to our gut feelings. How many times have you reflected on a situation and said, "I should have just listened to my gut"? Probably more times than you want to admit. Learning how to use your thoughts to compliment your gut feelings can be a very powerful tool and can help you make wise decisions. But how can you tell the difference between your emotional thoughts and your instinctual gut feelings? It takes time to develop these senses, especially if they have never been used. One way you can tell that your gut instinct is at work is when you hear yourself say, "Something just doesn't feel right." Another way to differentiate your emotional thoughts versus your gut instinct is to imagine you are walking home from work at night and you are extremely exhausted. As you approach the alleyway shortcut that saves you an extra two blocks you get a funny feeling. Your thoughts are telling you to take the shortcut because you are exhausted and you've done it a million times before. But at the same time, your gut feeling is telling you tonight is not the best night to walk through there. Bottom line—the more you get into the habit of paying attention to your emotional thoughts versus your gut feelings, it will get easier to tell the difference between the two.

REFLECTING

"When I started courting myself years ago I used meditation to help me relax and center myself. It is an amazing way to still your thoughts, relax your entire body, and feel connected to the deepest part of you. People always tell me that they can't meditate because they don't know how to still their thoughts; well meditation takes time and patience. It may take a few days, weeks or months to master it but once you do, you will get this amazing "high." My advice is to sit in a comfortable position on the floor or in a chair and close your eyes. Start with your toes and imagine they are limp and relaxed. Then imagine your feet, ankles, and calves are heavy and relaxed. Do this with each body part until you get to your head and this will help your body get very relaxed. Then, just sit there and be still for a few minutes. Do it every day or every few days until you have less and less mind clutter. Once you get to the point where the mind clutter goes away just sit there and be still. Some of my greatest ideas have come to me in meditation. If you want you can also add a scented candle and dimmed lighting or whatever makes you feel like you are in a relaxed environment."
~Ally

"Not making enough time for myself was a place I lived in for a long time. I was always giving and thinking that I would one day get around to myself. I thought I would have time for me as soon as I did all of these things right now for everyone else. Living like that made me feel like I had clipped my wings. The nature of my day was to get as many things done as I could but with little emotion, almost like I was on autopilot. Needless to say, I was unhappy, snappy, and may have even been abrasive at times. I lacked compassion and love for myself. I forgot what it was like to be gentle with others and myself. Maybe I even thought that there would be a reward from the universe if I showed that I could give of myself in a selfless way—always looking out for others. It worries me how my kids viewed me at that time in my life. Will it affect them down the road? Would I have been a little bit more of a better mother if I had been there for myself? I knew something had to give because I wanted to show my kids happiness and not just speak on it. The bottom line is that I felt like I was existing for a long time but not living. I finally started to remember to love myself and be gentle with me. I found ways to let go of the tension I was holding onto due to stress by reading quotes and literature to enlighten me. I found things that intrigued me visually. I started hugging my children more and talking to them instead of at them. I started looking up videos on my career (and working on this book). I started to internalize what I had not been practicing. It's been a journey and it's not over. But these are the subtle nuisances I began to acknowledge on my first date with myself. I began the journey to take the time to pay attention to the simple things that make my heart feel good and feel at ease and I am in a much better place because of it."

~Tara

FINDING YOUR HAPPY PLACE-PURSUING YOUR DREAMS & HAVING MORE FUN

By now, you've had at least one date night with yourself and you are learning about things you like or don't like, love and don't love about yourself. If so, then you are ready for the next phase. The Goddess Principle #2 is all about pursuing your dreams and having more fun. Having fun and exploring your creativity should not only be reserved for children or people in the arts. Adults far too often make life so serious and forget that balancing that inner joy and creativity is part of what makes us human. When you do things out of passion, you really can find your purpose.

AFFIRMATION

Look in the mirror and say:
*"I am beautiful. I am smart. I am
motivated to focus on my passions in
life and have fun while doing it."*

Step 1-TAP INTO YOUR INNER FIRE

People have different personalities and unique gifts
and that's a beautiful thing, but it's your inner fire that
gets things moving. Your inner fire guides and moti-
vates you to seek out the things you want and make
them happen. If you haven't tapped into it, you should.
The inner fire or spark is what drives you to start your
own business, or say "hi" to a guy you have a crush on.
Plus, when your inner fire is used in balance, it can also
help you know when and how to stand up for yourself.
This attribute comes in handy even when searching for
a job, or really doing anything. But when it's not used
in balance, it can distract you from getting you where
you want to be. To balance your fire, first start by rating
yourself. Are you low flame, medium flame (balanced),
or high flame? Once you figure out which one you are,
then start taking baby steps each day to be more in

the middle. For example, if you are low flame (shy, timid etc.) then do little things like start saying "hi" to strangers, which is probably out of your comfort zone. Or, if you are high flame and hot-tempered, then the next time you want to roll your eyes stop yourself and count to ten. Basically, make a conscious effort to bring it down a notch.

Step 2-OVERCOME PROCRASTINATION

Many people blame procrastination for the reasons they aren't getting things done. Procrastination is like a disease and if you don't stop it in its tracks it can spread and get you in a place where you feel like there is no point of return. The next time you are tempted to procrastinate from making your dreams come true, or from doing something else really important, remind yourself with a sticky note on your mirror that says, "Every moment is precious, use your time wisely—you will never get this moment back."

Step 3-HAVE A KINDERGARTEN SESSION

This may sound super-silly but in order for you to figure out what your passion is, or just to get into a creative mindset, sometimes you have to take it way back. Sit down somewhere comfortable, close your eyes and try to remember the things you enjoyed doing during your childhood. Were you the child who had paintings all over the fridge? Were you into building things a lot? Did you like to sit in the kitchen and watch your mom cook meals and come up with your own creations? Think about it and write down whatever words come to mind. This is not a technical assignment so try not to over-think it. Just write down five words that come to mind and if it helps pull out old pictures. Then, once you are done you can look at the words to see what types of things are written down and choose one to try first.

List Creative Childhood Activities:

1._____

2._____

3._____

4._____

5._____

Step 4-MAKE A LIFESTYLE CROSSWORD PUZZLE

Another activity that may help is a lifestyle crossword puzzle. List the things that give you a sense of purpose, the things you are good at, and the things you enjoy doing. Then, similar to a crossword puzzle, draw circles around groups of words that have common themes. Sometimes this is a great way to figure out your passion and possibly what type of job would be good for you if you were looking to switch careers.

SENSE OF PURPOSE	THINGS YOU ARE GOOD AT	THINGS YOU ENJOY

Step 5-TAKE A CLASS

Now that you have an idea of something creative or fun that you might like to do, it's time to actually try it out. For those of you who already are on the path to your dreams, taking a fun class still can't hurt, plus you never know who you will meet. Start by looking online for local workshops. You could also visit your local library to see what classes they have to offer. If there's nothing in your area, then start something on your own. If jewelry design is your passion, then gather a group of like-minded friends and start monthly meetings. In the meeting, you can watch online tutorials to create your own class and learn the basics together. The point is, don't give up on taking a class or being proactive just because the class isn't available in a way you deem convenient—be creative and make the best of your circumstances.

Step 6-WRITE YOUR DREAM DAY

If you could wake up tomorrow morning and have anything you wanted in the world what would it be? Write down your dream day story. You could start by introducing yourself, and then describe your perfect day and the types of things you do and have in your life.

What would your job be (if you had one)? Would you be married or single? Do you have kids? Are you traveling the world? Make this activity completely limitless and then let your instinct guide you on how to start creating this reality step by little step.

Write Your Dream Day:

_____

_____

_____

_____

_____

_____

_____

_____

_____

_____

_____

_____

_____

_____

_____

_____

Step 7-START USING VISUALIZATION

When you have a gala to attend, the first thing you might do is start to imagine what types of gowns you would wear. You think about the color, style, shoe options, and accessories. Then you go out looking for what you want and you make a purchase. Visualization for your life's dreams and aspirations works the same way. It is the mental imagery paired with clear intent and actions that help you get what you want. Using visualization is not a new concept, but it can definitely be a creative reminder of who you are and where you are going. Force yourself to take time out of your schedule to make a creative vision board. The great thing is that it can be whatever you want. It can be as big as a poster board or as small as an 8 x 10 piece of paper. When trying to figure out what to put on your board, don't get too technical. Just have fun and remember that when you look at it, it should make you feel good. If you want to buy a house, then print out a picture of your dream house and cut out pictures of furniture from a magazine along with positive quotes. Or if you have dreams of becoming a chef maybe you want to put a picture of a celebrity chef that inspires you, and pictures of dishes you love to make. You could also write restaurant reviews about yourself pretending you were a patron who loved the food you cooked. Even though the restaurant review is totally made up it can be a cute way to stay motivated. Try and spend time with the board every day, even if it's only a few minutes, because it's a way to connect with your vision.

Step 8- REMEMBER THOUGHTS & WORDS ARE POWERFUL

Have you ever wondered why people say you should speak things into existence? Positive thinking and positive speaking are great attributes to have, especially when you are pursuing a passion or just on the path towards a happier, healthier life. One example of how powerful words can be is an experiment that was done by Masaru Emoto. The Japanese author, researcher and entrepreneur did an experiment in 1994 where he decided to start freezing water to examine the frozen water molecules with a microscope. The result was that he observed beautiful crystals after giving good words, playing good music, or offering pure prayer to the water. He noticed disfigured molecules after giving negative words to the water. So the point is that the water itself was affected by the words. The parallel is that because humans are made mostly of water, it stands to reason that positive words probably affect the water molecules in our body in a good way and negative words probably affect the water molecules in our body in a bad way.

REFLECTING

"I started my own business when I was 9 years old making and selling jewelry. I am one of those serial entrepreneurs and I never had an issue coming up with ideas or getting started; it was procrastination and finishing projects that was always my issue. A few years ago after finally deciding to listen to my mom's advice, I decided to slow it down and focus on one project at a time. I realized I started to have more success with each venture. I noticed that by forcing myself to work on one thing at a time, I wasn't overwhelmed, I actually enjoyed the creative process, and I had more time to think about business development and longevity."

~Ally

"I always try to remember things that used to make me happy. When I was a young adult, I used to immerse myself in things that I loved and enjoyed and it was not about money but the richness of the feeling. Every now and then when I need some grounding or inspiration, I go back to exploring those things and I find them. I find them in art, in reading, in fulfilling the artistic side of me, or seeing a play where the work is outstanding. I search for things that are also meaningful to my soul. I seek out what my life is missing based on what I have experienced and I go there. I go alone so I'm not interrupted. It is just me filling this cup in my heart and awaking my senses so that I feel alive. Plus, I am learning to meditate and it's an awesome feeling. I know that a quiet and clear mind is imperative for tomorrow's success. I find a quiet place amongst all the chatter and I take these moments seriously. All of these things have helped me to also live in the moment because I've learned that happiness is not always when all is "right" but it's in the simple things that happen throughout the day."

~Tara

CLEANING HOUSE-REMOVING NEGATIVE PEOPLE, THOUGHTS & THINGS

When you make the decision to unleash your Goddess Potential there are people and things that must go. The worst thing you can do on a new, more positive journey is participate in things that don't add something positive to your life, or hang around people with an overall negative disposition. Sometimes you can't help it, because some of those "negative naysayers" might happen to be your mother or siblings. However, if it's possible, just take those people in doses. A 30-year study conducted by the Mayo Clinic found that optimists had a lower risk of early death than pessimists, which proves that striving towards optimism is a good thing.

AFFIRMATION

Look in the mirror and say:

*"I release my own negative thoughts,
as well as people and things that don't
add to my life. I now embrace a more
optimistic outlook in each situation."*

Step 1-REMOVE NEGATIVE THOUGHTS

Changing negative thinking does not occur right away. Why? Well, it took thousands of experiences to cumulatively create the negative conclusions you have about yourself or the world around you and that's heavily embedded in your brain. When you are your own biggest critic, it can be very unhealthy and lead to stress. Chronic stress brings on headaches, high blood pressure, aches and pains, infertility: well the list goes on and on. So what is the solution? Well, you can start by catching yourself in the moment. Ask yourself, "Am I choosing to be positive in this moment?" or "Am I serving my highest potential by thinking or saying this?" Just the process of catching yourself in the moment and having awareness about it can help change it.

Step 2- HUMBLE YOURSELF

Why is this important when it comes to Cleaning House? Well, your ego can either work for you or work against you. If your ego is sky-high, then it's safe to say that it probably works against you. If you have a huge ego it's like having an invisible veil and all information and other opinions that come through the veil get tainted by your ego and its agenda of self-preservation. Now, how do we get huge egos? We live in a society that says the more knowledge and material things we acquire the better we are. You're probably thinking, "Ok, so what is the problem? That's not a bad thing." Well, it's only a bad thing when someone has all of this knowledge, but can't apply it to his/her own personal transformation on the inside. It is an awesome thing to read, be educated and acquire professional titles; however, if you have these things without knowing your own root—your own spirit—then what is the point? A homeless man with no education, place to live, or any friends and family could be the wisest person in the world. Just because his life experiences have led him to his current status doesn't mean he isn't wise or doesn't know anything. And humbling yourself simply means that you acknowledge that is possible. In a similar vein, just because someone you know is fabulously well educated, wealthy, or powerful it does not mean that person has a good heart, or knows him or herself better. Humbling yourself brings your ego back down to a very basic and real level that allows you to have a little more compassion, which will allow you to empathically connect with different kinds of people.

Step 3- STOP COMPLAINING

How can you move forward on a new path while you complain about every little thing that annoys you? No one is exempt from complaining now and then, but when you complain, all it does is open the flood gates for more complaining which can lead to stress and affect your whole day or week. One way you can try to stop complaining is to set up a complaining detox where you can't complain about anything; not even the smallest thing; for three days. Whether it's the long line at your coffee shop, traffic, or that someone just annoyed the hell out of you, just force yourself to brush it off. Sometimes venting is necessary, but there are some smaller situations to which you need not give your energy. If you think about it, you really could be doing something more productive with your time. Instead, the next time you have a complaint just start getting into the habit of counteracting it with a solution. You will be shocked at how these small changes can slowly generate a more positive outlook.

Step 4-KEEP THE GOOD ONES

The people who you decide to keep in your life are not going to be perfect; however, they are around because you know at their core that they have your back and they add something to your life. They might be the ones who make you laugh, or with whom you can confide. Plus, you feel good when you are around them.

Step 5-LET SOME PEOPLE GO

Negative people are toxic and some are unaware of their toxic impact. However, some are completely aware and may even find satisfaction in creating chaos.

When you are around negative people, whether you like it or not, you absorb that energy in some way and it really can affect you. There is absolutely no need to keep naysayers, chronic complainers, and people who are just constantly unhappy about every single aspect of life around all the time. The best way to figure out who these folks are is to pay attention to how you feel after you leave their presence. Do you feel drained after that hour of dinner with them? If you feel drained, then either slowly wean these people out of your life, or just minimize the amount of time you spend around them. If they ask why, be honest and let them know you are taking "me" time.

Step 6-CLEAN & ORGANIZE

Unleashing your Goddess Potential is easier to do if you have an environment that is clean and peaceful to come home to every day. Creating a harmonious environment starts with creating a clutter-free environment. Start in little steps by taking out extra things that bulk up your home. Once a week or once a month, go room by room and see what needs to be thrown out or packed away in an organized labeled box in the basement or storage. If you don't have a lot of things to go through, then just make sure your personal space is at least organized and labeled in a way that makes it easy for you to find things. If you take pride in all of the things you have to do in life, even cleaning, then it makes it more enjoyable. And as a result, instead of viewing it as a "chore," you will look forward to it, because you know it will only make your life better. Once you are done getting organized, consider getting a scented candle, room spray, or an essential oil that you like. There are many benefits to an environment that smells awesome and the art of aromatherapy is the perfect example. According to the National Association for Holistic Aromatherapy, aromatherapy can be defined as the art and science of utilizing naturally extracted aromatic essences from plants to balance, harmonize and promote the health of body, mind and spirit. These fragrant therapeutic oils can be dispersed into your living space using an essential oil diffuser.

Here are some essential oil basics:

Lemon = stimulating
Lavender = relaxing

Peppermint = relieves fatigue

Jasmine = fights stress and anxiety

Sandalwood = calms nerves

The goal is for your personal space to look, feel, and smell good. And no worries; if getting organized is not naturally your thing, then ask a close friend or family member to help you get started.

Step 7-ANALYZE YOUR HABITS

Negative people and clutter aren't the only things in your life that could be holding you back from moving forward. Your habits fall into two categories: they are either good for you or bad for you. And if the bad ones become ruling influences, then there might be a chance you are addicted to them. It is up to you to determine the "healthy" and "unhealthy" habits and activities. Remember that the things you watch and participate in affect your mind, body, and spirit. If you like horror movies for example, pay attention to how you feel after watching a horror movie or a horror marathon. Do you feel drained? Do you feel motivated? Do you feel happy? This is not a judgment, just a reminder to pay attention to how you feel after you do certain things. Another example is if you always have drama with a co-worker. How do you feel when you come home from work? Do you feel drained? Do you feel good? What about Internet commenting or arguing? You would be surprised how many people argue in the comments section over articles on various topics. What about something like salsa dancing? Does it make you feel good? If so, you should do more of it! Just look at the activities in your life and figure out if you should lessen some of them a little or increase some of them. The point is that our experiences and environment help shape who we are and how we feel.

Step 8-TAKE A BREAK FROM ELECTRONICS

Have you ever gotten to a point on social media where you've had to set some folks status to "NO NOTIFICATION" because they post a lot of negative or emotional updates? Even though we may not know the author of the blog, or all the people in our Instagram or Facebook feed, we can absorb their energy just the same! Sometimes reading Facebook is like being on an emotional rollercoaster. Yes it's entertaining, fun, and funny to check your timeline every 10 to 15 minutes. And yes, your favorite show will be on in an hour and you just can't miss it. And yes, there is a breaking story on your favorite blog. This is not to say you shouldn't indulge in the fun stuff, it's just to suggest having a break from it once in a while. Making this a monthly habit and not a one-time thing allows you to relax your mind a little and focus on other things in your life.

REFLECTING

"I have been through the ringer when it comes to people taking advantage of my niceness. So I've spent the last five or six years making sure that the people I give my love, friendship, and attention to are deserving of it. It has been an up and down process but I've come to a point where I respect the ebbs and flows of friendships. It's ok that someone you thought would be a lifetime friend may not be that person anymore and it doesn't mean there is any ill will...it's just that you may not vibe anymore."

~Ally

"Cleaning house is an action. This action includes getting rid or letting go of all things that are not helping you be as productive as you need to be, as happy as you need to be, and hindering your growth. It has been so hard for me because it consists of evaluating my relationships with people that I love and I had to let go of this dream that my family is supposed to be or look a certain way. Letting go of that dream has been one of the biggest parts of my acceptance. So now I focus on what is most pure on a basic level and it starts with my kids. As a child, your mom is your universe and she teaches you all there is to know. I am focusing on being understanding, wise, and loving for them. I am taking pride in all I do for them. For me it has been one of the best feelings in the world because it has allowed me a place to start my journey to self-love! To simply love them and be loved feels awesome! Cleaning house has brought me down to the very basic root level of love. And what's nice for me is that I can also truly say I have not lost one friend since 'Love & Hip Hop' started. My circle of friends has always been very small and I did not allow that to change because of reality TV. All my real friends know my heart and they know the type of person I am."

~Tara

SELF-MASTERY & HEALING THE BODY TEMPLE

The journey to self-discovery must also include a discussion on being physically healthy. Body, mind, and spirit are all connected, so it makes sense that all three need to be in tune in order for all aspects of your life to fall in place. Think about how you view nature for a minute. Have you ever had times when you are driving down a scenic route and observed the beautiful red, brown, and yellow leaves on a tree? Or have you ever just sat back and taken in the warmth of the beautiful sun? Now, do you feel the same admiration for your body? Your body is made from those same elements in nature and yet we find those elements so intriguing when they are in nature but not when they are in us. According to a study published in the open access journal PLOS (Public Library of Science) Medicine, people who do the four things below live on average an additional 14 years, compared with people who adopt none of these behaviors:

1. Don't smoke,
2. Exercise,
3. Drink alcohol in moderation,
4. Eat five servings of fruits and vegetables per day.

AFFIRMATION

Look in the mirror and say:

"Inside and out, I am literally a beautiful reflection of nature. My body is a beautiful flourishing vessel of good health, love and peace. I respect her and I love her."

Step 1-ASK YOURSELF ARE YOU IN AN ABUSIVE RELATIONSHIP?

In this step you need to identify what type of relationship you currently have with your body. Are you in an abusive relationship with your body? Neglect, constant put-downs, toxic food, and toxic beauty could mean you are in an abusive relationship and don't even know it. Why is it important to make sure we aren't being abusive? The physical makeup of a woman is very special. Whether we choose to have kids or not, our bodies are still designed in a way that has allowed us to help create all human life on earth. When you think about that, it's pretty deep. So your body is this beautifully designed vessel that you get to use while on Earth and maybe it's time to think about how you treat it. There is only so much the human body can take in the form of abuse before it starts to rebel.

Step 2-UNDERSTAND THE SYMMETRY OF LIFE

The word "balance" is used frequently in life as a goal to achieve. But why is it important to have balance in your life and health? If you take a look around you, you will see there is symmetry or balance everywhere. The streets and highways have equal lines. The glasses you're wearing have equal sides. The chair you are sitting in has four equal legs so you can sit up straight. There are many things in nature and that we use in life that have a balance to them, so doesn't it make sense that you should give your body that same balance? That's why the body flourishes with balanced meals, balanced physical activity and a balanced mind free of constant stress.

Step 3-LEARN HOW TO MASTER YOUR EMOTIONS

The benefit to mastering your emotions is that it ultimately leads to less stress and can have a more positive effect on your physical body. There is a quote by Aristotle that says "Anyone can become angry – that is easy, but to be angry with the right person at the right time, and for the right purpose and in the right way – that is not within everyone's power and that is not easy." Many people go through life on an emotional rollercoaster of ups and downs and a person's emotions can be their downfall. If you are too emotional, you get offended all the time and it can cause friction between you and everyone with whom you interact. If you aren't emotional enough, you can come off cold and push away people who love you the most. You will probably spend your lifetime trying to create a balance between the two, but trying and working towards it is half the battle. There is definitely a time to be sad and a time to be happy and a time to be excited. Mastering your emotions first means identifying how emotional you are, and if you don't know already then ask some close friends for an assessment. Tell them you promise not to take it too personally but you are working on self-growth and want their honest opinion on how emotional they think you are and what they think about your other character traits. If possible, have them put it in writing so you can refer back to it for reflection purposes. Then, just start to be your own observer the next time you are emotional.

Step 4-CONNECT WITH NATURE

How can you heal your body if you don't even know what it's made of? Just because you didn't major in biology or study to become a doctor doesn't mean that you shouldn't know anything about your own body. When healing your body, if you know what it's made of, appreciate it, connect with the elements of it, then there is a possibility that the effects of your healthy journey might last longer. Almost 99% of the mass of the human body is made of six elements: oxygen, carbon, hydrogen, nitrogen, calcium, and phosphorus.

Here are ways to connect with nature:

Name: Oxygen/Nitrogen
In the body: Your body needs oxygen for energy and to keep your cells alive. Nitrogen is an important part in your DNA and your body needs it to make proteins in your muscles, skin, and hair.
In nature: Found in air.
Suggestion: Deep breathing exercises.

Name: Carbon
In the body: The element carbon is not in its pure form in the body, but it is found as a compound and it is the basic building block that forms proteins, carbohydrates and fats.
In nature: Found in sunlight.
Suggestion: Sunbathe or make sure your blinds are open during the day.

Name: Hydrogen
In the body: Hydrogen in the body is a component that makes up water and water makes up over 60 percent of the human body.
In nature: Found in water.
Suggestion: Drink more water or take a calm bath.

Name: Calcium

In the body: Calcium in the body is the main constituent of bones.

In nature: Found in rocks and seashells.

Suggestion: Collect beautiful rocks or seashells and keep them around your house or office.

Step 5-TRY A DETOX

The best time to start a new healthy lifestyle is right after a detox. Toxins store up in your body, slow it down and make you unhealthy over time. Detoxing is one of the best ways to remove toxins from the body. These toxins can come from a variety of factors that include the food you eat, your environment, and the stress in your life. There are many ways to detox including juice fasts, water fasts, veggie fasts and many others. If you have never done a detox before, you should consider working with your doctor or holistic practitioner to get started and find out what they suggest based on your diet and lifestyle. And remember to also look up side-effects of detoxing, because as the body rids itself of toxins sometimes it creates the common cold, aches and pains, or even headaches as the body gets all the bad stuff out. The benefits of detoxing could leave you feeling lighter, having more energy, and having more concentration. Detoxing also helps to flush and cleanse your organs, helps rid the body of unhealthy parasites, helps to clear the body of free radicals, and helps clean the blood. Overall detoxing can help you jumpstart your way into a healthier lifestyle, because most times unhealthy cravings aren't as strong after you detox.

Step 6-COMMIT TO AT LEAST ONE HEALTHY FOOD A DAY

Imagine that your body is a car. If you forget to do oil changes, put cheap gas in it, and never take it for a tune-up, what happens? Your car may stop in the middle of the road and never start again. But the bottom line is, no matter how shiny your car looks on the outside, if on the inside it's all messed up and not taken care of, eventually it could lead to severe issues. And unlike a car, you can't just buy a new human body. While you are going to work, listening to music, talking on the phone, laughing, and having fun, your body is working like clockwork on the inside to keep running. There is a glorious process going on inside you and that process thrives on foods that serve as fuel.

Some good fuel foods you could try incorporating are:

1. Vegetables: celery, kale, sweet potatoes, spinach, broccoli, carrot sticks
2. Nuts: almonds, walnuts, peanuts, pecans, pistachios (roasted and unsalted)
3. Fruit: avocado, bananas, apples, prunes, oranges, mangoes, strawberries, blueberries, figs
4. Seeds: sunflower seeds, sesame seeds, whole or ground flaxseeds
5. Beans: black, kidney, garbanzo, lentils, split peas

How many of us incorporate a few of these in our diets daily? If you don't already, then start simple and try one a day. If you know you aren't a big fruit eater, then maybe try a smoothie and see if you like the taste. If you know you don't like salads, then try a veggie stir-fry with beans. If you could get to a point where your kitchen is viewed as a healing center then your body will rejoice.

The right food can help give you an amazing amount of natural energy each day, can sharpen the mind, and help you be less edgy even under stress, plus it can taste good too. In addition to eating healthier, try and stay active in simple ways. Take the stairs more, go for a daily fifteen-minute walk or bike ride, or take a dance class once a week with your girls—just get moving.

Step 7-HAVE A LOOK AT WHAT YOU PUT ON YOUR BODY

You can drive yourself crazy if you try to read every single ingredient on every lotion, deodorant, shampoo, nail polish, lipstick, body wash or toothpaste, but it doesn't hurt to pay a little more attention to what's going on your body. Toxic products are no myth and your skin is your largest organ; sometimes we don't even pay attention to how we treat it. Educate yourself on some of the toxic ingredients, so you know what key words to look for in cosmetic products. There are even websites that list brands free of toxic ingredients to make it easy for you. The Campaign For Safe Cosmetics has been working with companies to make products safer for over seven years. And there is an app called "Think Dirty" with over 68,000 products listed; such knowledge empowers and educates the consumer on the cosmetics industry by allowing buyers to make informed decisions.

Step 8-UNITE WITH YOUR FEMININE ESSENCE POWER

Some people call this "womb power" but whatever you want to call it, it's important to remember that your womb and reproductive system is a sacred part of your body. A woman's uterus and vagina have helped contribute to all life on Earth. Now, our wombs are no longer viewed as sacred and how we view menstruation is a good example of that. Many people, including women, have been taught to view menstruation as something gross and annoying. Did you know that your menstrual blood could have healing powers? Menstrual blood is rich in stem cells. Stem cells in the body can heal a wide variety of diseases. Researchers are currently making the connection between these menstrual stem cells and heart disease, Parkinson's, diabetes and more. This is not to promote blood donating, but to show you how important that blood and process really is in the body. We should also pay attention to the chemicals we put in our vagina through things like tampons. Think about it, if you are thirty years old and you started your period at twelve years old, it means that you have had your period for 216 months with the potential use of over 1700 pads and tampons. That adds up to be a lot of chemicals! There are tampon brands without chemicals like chlorine. They are made with certified organic cotton, free of fragrance and dyes. Sometimes these brands are one or two dollars more expensive, but if you can afford it, look at it as an investment in your health. Plus ladies, we can't get mad if men or society have no respect for our bodies when we don't even view our own wombs as sacred. You don't have to make a shrine for your womb, but just acknowledge her and start to have respect for your feminine essence. That alone can be powerful. There is a quote by Dario Salas Sommer in his book, *Does Woman Exist* that talks about nurturing your femininity: "More than anything, a woman needs to become the 'mother of herself', focusing her maternal capacity towards her own person, place herself under her own care, and verse herself in the art of femininity."

REFLECTING

"I have struggled with my sugar addiction and extra weight ever since the birth of my twin boys and they are three now. It took me about six months to break a coffee addiction (the same way it did for me to stop putting chemical relaxers in my hair) that I had for about two years. The last straw was when I started having pains in my left breast and my menstrual cycle didn't come. My instinct told me it had to be my diet. Coffee and sweet things were my go-to junk when I would get a little stressed. Sometimes being a twin mommy has its moments and that's how I handled my little moments of stress. But I was having aches, I had an attitude and I knew something had to give. So I took it (and am still taking it) one step at a time. First I cut coffee cold turkey for almost 4 weeks. And although I started drinking it again, I don't drink it as much and the cravings are less and less. And then I thought, "Ok, I have the coffee part down pat, now how will I conquer my sugar addiction?" I am one of those people that love all things sweet and it's basically a recipe for disaster if you want to be healthy and lose weight like me. So now I'm making sure that at least my dinner is super healthy everyday. And what I've noticed is that the more I start to slowly incorporate healthier food, the less I crave the candy bars. Anyway it's a process, I'm just happy that I had that small amount of willpower to listen to my body when it was screaming at me to change."

~Ally

"Staying fit and healthy is very important for me because we already have all of these mental stresses. If I ever have extra time, instead of wasting that hour, I just work out. It keeps my endorphins going and puts me in such a good mood. My daily routine usually consists of working out when the kids are playing. I would do 30 laps up and down my stairs and in between those laps if I was fatigued I would take my 50-second break and then I would do squats. I would also have the weights at the top of the stairs. Plus, the park that we go to has a little bit of workout equipment and I would also find a brick and do squats with that brick. What I've realized about children is they don't venture very far from their mother. They are at the age where they want to be close to me so that makes it easier for me to work out in the park. If I had to break up my workout and I could only do cardio in the park then when I put them to bed I would go online and search for a 30-minute Ab or a 30-minute core workout. For me it's like once I started working out, I felt like how did I live my life without doing this before...I really enjoy it. The overall point is that self-mastery and healing your body starts with dedicating yourself to a positive routine and that means forcing yourself even when you don't feel like it. The physical is just as important as the mental and all of it's going to take some effort on your behalf."

~Tara

WHAT ABOUT LOVE?

Why are finding love, learning how to keep good love, knowing when to release someone you love, and knowing how to deal with a bad breakup important things to talk about when developing a relationship with your inner self? Exploring the topic is important, because the way we act in romantic relationships is really just a projection of what's going on inside of us anyway…the two are closely tied. According to Statisticbrain.com and their online dating stats, "71 percent of people believe in love at first sight."

AFFIRMATION

Look in the mirror and say:
*"I radiate pure and unconditional
love. I deserve to be treated with
respect from my partner."*

Step 1- BE AWARE OF THE PRINCESS SYNDROME

How many times have you seen a little girl dressed as a princess? Whether it's for Halloween or a birthday party, there are a lot of little girls who want to be a princess and who fall in love with the idea of a fairytale love. That idea about love can last throughout adulthood for some women. Why is this idea detrimental to a woman who wants love? Because, every single woman is not going to magically and in a mystical way bump into her soul mate on the street and live happily ever after. If you happen to be a woman who believes that love is supposed to happen like a fairytale, ask yourself is this idea about love working for you? If it is, that's awesome, but if it's not, you should try letting it go. Find ways to remind yourself that people meet in all types of ways and those situations can be just as special.

Step 2-LEARN HOW TO ATTRACT LOVE

Who doesn't want to feel loved, respected, cherished and appreciated by someone else? That's not to say that love should be constantly on everyone's mind 24/7, but who do you know that has never ever wanted to feel loved and needed by someone at some point? It is a very natural and beautiful human need. Why does it seem so hard at times to find true love? When you explore your own nature, learn to love who you really are at your core and develop a trusting relationship with yourself you can create a well-lit pathway to attract "Mr. Right." If you are looking for a certain kind of mate, then you have got to make sure you have those same qualities first and this could take some time. Once you feel you're ready, and you've taken the right steps then just like a magnetic force you will attract someone who is the right fit.

Step 3-STEP OUT OF YOUR COMFORT ZONE

Once you have started to slowly de-program your princess syndrome (if you deem necessary), you can get to the fun part and that's meeting your mate. When you unleash your Goddess Potential you are getting in touch with your soul and you have to be in touch with your soul to meet your soul mate. Now, let's pretend for a minute that you want to start a business and you have the faith that your dreams will come true. You get your company registered, get business cards, write a business plan, and figure out how to get clients. Now, how come when it comes to love, some of you think you can sit there and it will fall into your lap? Just like you have to make an effort with other things such as school and business, you also have to put an effort into finding love. Effort doesn't mean being pressed; it just means being open and stepping out of your comfort zone a little. That could mean many things depending on the person. For one woman, it may mean trying out a dating website, matchmaking service, or speed dating. For someone else, it could mean putting herself in a new environment. That new environment could be a cooking class or a festival. And if you have a usual "type" in mind, that doesn't mean you can't step outside the box and be open to dating other kinds of people. As long as they respect you and you are attracted to them in some way, then why not give it a chance? Albert Einstein said "Insanity: doing the same thing over and over again and expecting different results." So, why not try something new?

Step 4-IDENTIFY YOUR STANDARDS & MAKE A PERFECT MATE LETTER

Part of meeting the "one" is identifying what ideas you have about love and why you have them. Just because you believe something about love doesn't mean it's working for you or it's in your best interest to keep thinking that way. It's obviously up to you what you think is important but remember that quality of character is an awesome thing for a man to have. It's better to focus on his core and his character than his material possessions or accomplishments, because at the end of the day the man with character is the one who will be by your side through thick and thin. Now write down your standards you look for in an ideal mate.

List five things that should always be present in a loving relationship:

1._____
2._____
3._____
4._____
5._____

List five qualities that are non-negotiable for your ideal partner:

1._____

2._____

3._____

4._____

5._____

Now you are ready for your mate letter. Put yourself in a relaxed mode one evening with tea or soft music or by lighting a few candles. Then take your pen and paper, close your eyes, and imagine yourself filled with love. With your eyes closed, imagine this love energy starting at your feet and working its way up your entire body until it surrounds you. Then start writing out your list, or develop a short story about the mate you want to attract. Take the letter, fold it, put it in an envelope and seal it with a kiss (with or without lipstick). Then take it and put it in an important safe place inside your house. The point of this activity is for the letter to serve as a positive reminder that love is on the way (being delivered, etc,).

Step 5-ENGAGE IN RANDOM ACTS OF KINDNESS

If random acts of kindness are already a part of your life, then that's awesome, because if you want to attract love, then you have to give love to others. If you don't usually partake in random acts of kindness, here are some things to consider. Make sure that you are currently treating the special people in your life with love and respect. Let them know how much you love and appreciate them in small ways with a greeting card, e-card, or just a simple text with a few kind words. And in addition to the people you know, why not reach out and touch strangers. Say "hi" to someone on the street or volunteer during the holidays at shelters. You could also volunteer at an orphanage or a big sister mentoring program. Another great way to give love is to compliment your fellow sisters. If you see a woman with a nice outfit, hairstyle, or something else, give her a compliment, because you never know who might need that compliment at that moment.

Step 6-REMEMBER NO ONE IS PERFECT & EVERY MAN IS UNIQUE

Sometimes we give up too fast on relationships. Remember that each man is unique and has unique experiences that have shaped him. Just because your best friend's man gives her flowers monthly, pays her bills, and gives her a weekly massage doesn't mean your man isn't a "good" one because he doesn't do those things. There is a quote by Theodore Roosevelt that says "Comparison is the thief of joy," so try to stay out of the habit of making relationship comparisons; they are a complete waste of time and not fair to your mate. Once you meet that special someone or even if you have been with him for years, it's important to constantly remember that he is not perfect. Sometimes it's easy to judge our mate while we tend to forget that we ourselves have made tons of mistakes, too. Obviously, you shouldn't allow anyone to degrade you, or physically abuse you but some of the lighter issues a man may have are worth at least trying to understand and be compassionate about if you think he is actually worth it.

Step 7-GIVE TLC TO THE RIGHT PERSON

Relationships are complex and there isn't just "one" right answer when it comes to matters of the heart. But when you find the one, or if you have been with him for a while now, it's good to remember to give him the tender loving care he deserves. Depending on his personality and the things he likes, give him little reminders here and there of how much you care. On the other hand, if you aren't sure if you are in a relationship that you should leave, make a checklist of pros and cons. If the cons heavily outweigh the pros then you might want to consider a serious conversation with your mate. If things don't get better, you may even want to consider taking a brief time period apart to reevaluate what's important to you both. Many of us have probably been in an unhealthy relationship at some point and it can be difficult because just like any other addiction, you can also be addicted to a certain type of man who doesn't treat you right.

Step 8-LEARN HOW TO COPE WITH A BAD BREAKUP

Ok, so what happens when love takes a turn for the worst? What do you do when you find yourself completely devastated from a breakup with someone you were head over heels in love with? This is the kind of heartache that penetrates deep and in some cases you cannot eat, sleep, or function in your normal way. Now what? The first thing you can do is allow yourself to grieve. Holding back feelings of hurt and sorrow from a breakup is unhealthy. Allow yourself to cry, be sad, and stare at the wall for a while. But while you are grieving, say this: "I've been single before, I can be single again," and say it every day. That one phrase can be the starting point for healing, because it's the truth. You were single before this relationship and you've probably survived other breakups and you will also survive this one. Through your grieving, confide in someone you trust and let it all out. Talk about life, talk about your insecurities and the things you're scared about. Having at least one person in your life that you can be completely vulnerable with can really come in handy during a bad breakup.

REFLECTING

"I truly in my heart of hearts believe that my husband is my soul mate. A few months before we met, I made a decision to not let my past heartaches affect my present and I decided I was ready and wanted love. I remember praying to God and saying "I have so much love to give." I asked that God help me remain open to love. So I decided to try online dating, research speed-dating events, and go out with friends more. I was being open and just going with the flow. Then on two different occasions I received a brochure in the mail about visiting Grenada. And I wasn't sure why at the time, but instead of throwing them away I kept them both. Two weeks later I ended up meeting my Grenadian soul mate on the subway and we have been together ever since."

~Ally

"I still believe in love and the power of it. I also live knowing what it is like to have lost it and been hurt by its absence. I know what it feels like to experience the deep pain that comes along with loving someone that has hurt you and they are not capable of fixing the pain and it's not an easy thing. Although it's hard I realize now that I have to force myself in baby steps to love smarter, with eyes open. I know that love heals the pain and mends the broken heart. It's the only thing that cannot be replaced by anything other than what it is, so that's why right now I am doing something simple - I am learning to love myself. I know that if I want to meet the "one" and have a good man in my life one day that it starts with me first. I am looking at myself and accepting and loving all of me. Flaws are no reason to beat yourself up or punish ourselves. I'm loving myself when I'm angry or if I say something stupid or simply don't show my full potential. And it also helps when I take moments to meditate on loving myself. When the lights are out, my phone is off and before I close my eyes I embellish in that feeling of love. Love does not need to be sought after or only given through external sources but it is right within you. This is where the healing of the heart comes from and I am preparing myself for another to love me as a whole and complete person."

~Tara

A DIALOGUE WITH YOUR WOUNDED SELF

At some point on your path to unleashing your Goddess Potential, you may need to do some uncomfortable digging. You have to dive headfirst into a very uncomfortable territory—your wounded self. Some people choose therapy to move on from the pain and trauma of the past, but if you aren't in therapy you still need to face past pain in order to move forward. Sometimes the part of you that has been hurt and betrayed can take on a life of its own and affect your romantic relationships, how you parent, and how you interact with people in many different situations. You may not even be aware that the chip on your shoulder is from when you were thirteen. When you let your past affect your present, your past rules your life. You should pat yourself on the back, because you are at an amazing stage of maturity in your life when you can begin to analyze yourself rationally and objectively. Remember to be gentle with yourself at this stage, too. According to the statistics found at PTSD United, Inc. "70% of adults in the U.S. have experienced some type of traumatic event at least once in their lives. This equates to approximately 223.4 million people."

AFFIRMATION
Look in the mirror and say:
"I am strong enough to tackle my past pain.
I know that just because I've been hurt it
doesn't mean I have to stay hurt. I have
confidence that I can move forward."

Step 1-REALIZE WHAT THE OPEN WOUND DOES

An emotional wound from past pain is just like an open wound to the body. A wound on the body that never heals increases the risk for infection, which can lead to serious conditions and possibly even the loss of a limb. And if the emotional open wound never heals, it festers almost like a disease and can manifest in many different ways, causing havoc in your life. The open wound plays itself out in your current life from certain triggers. It can sometimes cause you to overreact to small things. Psychiatrist and author Dr. Keith Ablow did a wonderful job explaining how repressing past trauma can also lead to denial. He wrote, "Indeed, we accept the notion that the mind uses many defense mechanisms to distance us from bitter realities—we repress our emotions, we rationalize our behaviors, we distort past events. Chief among these mechanisms is denial, in which we unconsciously ignore distressing facts about ourselves or others. Denial can make us look the other way in the face of evidence that our marriages need help or that our business strategies need revamping. It can make us immune to feedback from friends, loved ones, or coworkers who warn us about our self-defeating behaviors."

Step 2-RECOGNIZE REPEATED LIFE PATTERNS

Becoming aware of repeated life patterns can aid in the process to healing your wounded self, because some of those patterns may not be good for you. You may not even realize that some of your repeated choices and habits are actually happening over and over again until you sit back and think about it. The same recurring theme of trauma will continue to play itself out until you have dealt with it.

Step 3-START YOUR RELEASE NOTES

Writing about the past pain can be very therapeutic. Write down all of the words that describe you when you feel down on the left side. Some things to ask yourself to get to these words might be: Are you insecure? Do you feel depressed? Do you feel hurt? Then in the middle put what types of things you think trigger those emotions. Then in the right column put what caused the pain. Was it something from childhood or a bad breakup that was never resolved? If you are having a hard time figuring out what specifically has caused some of your pain, reflect for a few days about your childhood, or past experiences.

THE FEELING	WHAT TRIGGERS IT	WHAT CAUSED IT

Step 4-ALLOW YOUR EMOTIONS TO FLOW

The reason people don't like to deal with past wounds is because doing so makes them feel as if they are re-living the moment and it's easier in the short run to just shove it under the rug somewhere. Through this pro-cess don't hold back what comes naturally. If you want to cry or sob, then do it, if you want to scream, scream. And if you want to throw a few things around (as long as you don't hurt yourself or anyone else) then do it. Because you have repressed the pain and emotions in various ways for so long, it's necessary to let out the feelings that come along with that pain.

Step 5-LEARN TO FORGIVE

Once you have identified the core issues and can pinpoint what or who caused them, then work on the next part in your release journey, which is forgiving. Writing and working on this part could take two months or ten years, but as long as baby steps are being taken towards forgiving, that's all that matters. Start by writing your own release affirmation. It could say something like, "I forgive (insert name) for (insert incident) that happened in (insert year). I forgive them because the past is gone and I won't allow it to cripple my future. I live only in the present and I realize that through compassion and understanding for other people's faults I can find healing."

Write Your Own Release Affirmation:

_____

_____

_____

Then the next step is to confront the person (if it was a person) who caused your pain. If there is a specific person who has caused your pain, then you may want to consider talking with them at some point. Now, this doesn't apply to all situations. If, for example, you just got out of a domestic violence situation, obviously you shouldn't meet back up with the person because it's not safe. But if it's a safe environment and if you think it will really help with your healing, then reach out to the person to see if they are willing to talk. But don't go into the experience expecting an apology or a certain outcome, because it's completely unpredictable. Instead, be proud of yourself for having the guts to reach out in the first place and tell yourself you will be ok no matter how it turns out. If confronting the person is not possible, you can still forgive them in your own mind and heart, because it will still help you in the end.

Step 6-HAVE A FEAR FUNERAL

Having a dialogue with your wounded self may be one of the hardest things you ever do, but once you start exploring it, the next thing to tackle is fear. Fear and worry go hand in hand with pain. And fear can be the most debilitating thing ever. Fear makes you question almost every decision you have to make. It can make you over-think and analyze your relationships, your career, your worth, your material things and every other aspect of your life. In *The Essence of Success* by Earl Nightingale he discusses statistics on worrying that say forty percent of the things you worry about will never occur anyway. What if, just what if, you acted like fear didn't exist? What if you made a conscious decision right now to let go of fear and have it never return? Well, obviously it's a process, but why not start with a fear funeral. Everywhere you see the parenthesis you enter these things: 1-Hometown, 2-Date, 3-Your first and last name, 4-Your age, 5-Your first name.

(1.   ) FEAR, died on (2.   ) at 5:48 PM following a brief illness.

FEAR leaves behind (3.   ), companion of (4.   ) years.

Born and raised in and around me, FEAR's life has come to an end. I willingly release FEAR and ask FEAR to never return. I have no need for FEAR any longer.

May FEAR rest in peace,
(5.   )

Step 7-LEARN TO SAY I'M SORRY

You may not realize it, but sometimes you also owe one person or many people in your life an apology, but your ego is too big, or time has passed and it may have slipped away from you. Being wrong about something and not acknowledging or apologizing will hold you back from moving forward and can contribute towards your own open wound. Sometimes it could even be a situation where you are too hard on yourself all the time and you may owe yourself an apology.

Step 8-HAVE A NEW OUTLOOK ON COMPASSION

On your journey to digging deeper and releasing some of your pain from your past, it's also important to remember that some of the people you encounter are probably wounded in some way, too. While you may be working on your dialogue with your wounded self, it doesn't mean that the rest of the world is. There is a quote by the English poet Samuel Taylor Coleridge that says, "What comes from the heart, goes to the heart." It's a gentle reminder that you may need someone to be compassionate towards you, so remember to give out compassion too.

REFLECTING

"Dealing with past pain has been and still is difficult for me. In my adult life, I spent a few years being mad that my father wasn't in my life and that no one ever talked to me about him. I was also mad that no one, not my mother or any other woman in my family talked to me about men or relationships. No one talked to me about boys or how they should treat me, about sex, or about any other real life topic. I learned everything from trial and error. I ended up in a few psychologically abusive relationships in my teen years and in my early adulthood. However, every "stupid" decision I ever made led me to this moment right here and I have zero regrets. I needed all of my crazy experiences to help me learn and make connections. So as a result of this "learn as I go" stuff, I actually ended up with a man who treats me like a queen. He's not perfect but he adores me, has a genuine spirit and I believe he truly has my back. Plus, what helped is when I realized that sometimes when you are growing up the reason the adults in your life can't guide you about something is because they don't know about it themselves. Maybe their parents never talked to them or maybe they happened to be in a bad relationship and felt they couldn't offer good guidance."

~Ally

"I've had my fair share of dark days where I've felt like I'm literally waking up each day in my own nightmare. I've also battled depression and terrible pain from things that have happened to me. So I started to remind myself little by little each day that I am stronger than the situations that happen in life and I made a conscious choice to not let situations keep me down. I read once in my own process that your emotional wounds have to be cleaned and patched daily, just as a physical wound has to be. Now what works for me is to write out how I feel and I affirm what I need to be feeling. I seek encouragement from higher beliefs for guidance on healing. I now try my best to live in the moment and believe in my affirmations and accept them to be true in my life. I now live knowing that I do have control and power over what I think and how I view myself. I also feel that seeking therapy to help put things in perspective can be a part of your healing process. Ultimately it comes down to learning how to let go and be honest with myself. Some days those old feelings of pain do arise and they aren't easy to ignore. When this happens I drill good words, reflect on good experiences, listen to good soothing music, and sometimes meditate to keep me or put me back on track."

~Tara

COPING WITH CHANGE

Change is inevitable, but what do you do when the change is not positive? What do you do in your lowest, darkest moments? What if your boyfriend of eight years dumps you for another woman? What do you do when you lose your house and your job, all in a three-month time period? If it seems like the world is drowning you, what do you do? Many people get stressed from these life-altering circumstances and according to research from the Statistic Brain Research Institute, 77 % of all people regularly experience physical symptoms caused by stress and 73% regularly experience psychological symptoms caused by stress.

AFFIRMATION

Look in the mirror and say:
"I can get through this. I will get through this because anything is possible. This situation in front of me will not determine the rest of my life." Then close your eyes and calmly say, "It's already ok," as many times as you need to.

Step 1-CHANGE YOUR PERSPECTIVE

The key to not falling apart every time something "bad" happens is to change your perspective in the moment. Your car breaks down and maybe the old you would have had a mini-meltdown, in which you would call your friends to curse and vent about it. Another way to handle it would be to take a deep breath and ask yourself, "Ok, what is the next thing to calmly do in this situation so that I can continue on with my day?" The point is to slowly get out of the habit of allowing one situation to make the rest of your day doom and gloom.

Step 2-HAVE AN OPEN MIND

People who have a hard time accepting small and large changes that occur in their lives should take into consideration that being more open-minded might help. Think about it; a closed mindset on different things in life just further perpetuates a mindset that is resistant to change when it occurs in life.

Step 3-CHANGE HOW YOU VIEW REJECTION

What if the door being shut in your face; not getting the job you applied for, or being told "no" time after time, was really an awesome thing? What if you viewed it that way? What if you got to a point in your life where rejection had absolutely no impact on you? You could just brush it off, see if there is anything to learn from it and move forward. It may be way easier said than done, but here's one way to look at it. Pretend you are looking down at your life from the sky. From that viewpoint you can see it all. You can see how all the roadblocks, opportunities, people you will meet, and experiences are moving and re-shaping constantly to get you to your goals. For example, you would be able to see from the sky that the man living a few miles from you just accepted a new job in London. He has to move his whole family there in a few months. When his wife puts in her two weeks at her job, you will be the one to fill her old position and end your two-year run of rejections and job searching. Even though you don't live in the sky to see these things working, it doesn't mean you can't keep in mind that the "no's" in life are necessary and important.

Step 4-REMEMBER LIFE CHANGES WHAT YOU WON'T

So, you have been working at your job for ten years but always wanted to be an artist who creates beautiful paintings. You never made it a priority. You end up losing your job abruptly and after the shock, you pull yourself together, temporarily sign up for unemployment while you look for work, and somehow surprisingly get the guts to take a painting class once a week. The point is, when you yearn for something on the inside and you aren't willing to make the changes on the outside to bring it into reality, then sometimes life will do it for you. Life will fire you from a job you hated anyway, make your boyfriend break up with you when you know you should have left years ago, and the list goes on. The point is, some negative change is avoidable if you start listening to your instinct and making the changes before life does it first.

Step 5-WRITE DOWN YOUR STRESS

Take a piece of paper and write down all of the things that are making you feel like crap on the left side of the sheet. And on the right side, write your idea for a solution or search online for each thing to see what others suggest to do. Then when you have some down time, find a quiet place, take a couple deep breaths and say "I release" whatever is on the left side and say: "I embrace" whatever is written on the right side directly across from it. This way you are saying out loud that you are releasing the stress and embracing the solution. Afterwards throw the paper away.

Step 6-CHANGE YOUR PASSWORD

Change your password to something like "BEOK2016" and make sure you don't have it set on automatic. Make sure that every time you log into your social media, you have to type it in so it serves as a constant reminder that you will get through the hard times. Just think back to something you dealt with years ago that you don't even think about anymore. It eventually got easier, right? Plus, can you think of anything you learned from it, or a person you met because of it?

Step 7-REMEMBER GRATITUDE CAN SET YOU FREE

When our circumstances change for the "worse", naturally we are not thinking about being thankful. But that could be one way out of a slump. You may, or may not, have a long list of things, but you can start by being thankful that you woke up another day. Do you have a place to live? Do you have a car? Do you have good health? Do you have a job? Do you have one or two really good friends who have your back? These may sound super-simple, but there are people who don't have any of these things.

Step 8-APPRECIATE ELDER WISDOM

Elder wisdom is unfortunately a lost concept today. It seems like there is an overall lack of respect and admiration for our elders. Who are your elders? Your elders are your parents, grandparents, or anyone who has been on this planet much longer than you. They aren't perfect, but it's a fact that just because of age alone they have had a lot of life experiences and may be able to offer pearls of wisdom. Those pearls will come from their mistakes and their success. And when you are down and out, they are the best people to talk to, because more than likely they have experienced job loss or heartbreak just like you. For example, if you know a couple that has been happily married for fifty years, why not listen to their relationship advice? It may help you and can make them feel needed. If you don't have any elders in your life, volunteer at an elderly home, because there are many elders there who would love to listen, share and feel appreciated.

REFLECTING

"When I chose to be a writer I knew my life, at least career-wise would always be full of change. I am so used to change now that I can be working one freelance writing gig for a year or two and when they call me out of the blue to tell me they don't need me, I literally feel nothing. I barely feel any emotion about it. And like clockwork I give myself a day to relax and then start looking for the next job, opportunity, or figure out a game plan. I believe that being this way helped me a lot the first few years raising twin boys as a first time mom. Twin mommy life is so unpredictable that if I hadn't been used to change, I think I would have been way more stressed."

~Ally

"There are two things that have helped me a little when it comes to coping with change. Being less judgmental towards myself and being a patient person has helped me stay calm. When things pop up that are unexpected, I try not to beat myself up about it and remember that if I'm patient the right opportunity will present itself. I have especially had these challenges when it comes to my love life. I've had to remind myself over and over that when it comes to love you are not going to do everything right all the time and it's ok."

~Tara

CONSISTENCY IS KEY

Once you develop a relationship with your inner self it never goes away—almost like learning to ride a bike. However, just like riding, it can become a little rusty if you haven't done it in ten years. Life experiences, social media, and being super-busy can make it hard to stay consistent with a healthy new lifestyle. For some, it may be easy to keep it going for six months or a year and for others it may be hard to keep it up for a week. So how can you keep your relationship with your inner self a flourishing one? Your relationship with self is still a relationship like any other and if you start to neglect it and forget about it, it will suffer. There is something called Implementation Intentions and the concept has to do with the strong effects of simple plans to keep goals and habits steady. For example, instead of saying, "I'm going to eat healthier," you could use Implementation Intentions in specific steps and say, "When I get home I will have a salad, then make my stir fry, then do a quick workout." It's the same goal but a simple change in how you get to the goal—that's the key to keeping good habits going for the long run.

AFFIRMATION

Look in the mirror and say:
"I am always rooted in self-love, balance and peace. As I move through life I will try my hardest to stay true to who I am at all times, but promise not to judge myself too harshly if I don't."

Step 1-LEARN HOW TO APPRECIATE THE EBBS AND FLOWS

The first thing you can do is try not to beat yourself up when you fall off from feeling centered and balanced. The point of the human experience is to have ebbs and flows. Think about it; positive and negative work together to give you a point of reference in this human life experience. How can you know what's really good without having some bad things happen? So instead of beating yourself up, remember that every day is an opportunity for a fresh start and just start mastering the art of bounce back. You can even use this book and start from Principle #1 all over again if that will help.

Step 2-COMMIT TO SOMETHING SIMPLE

Ok, so who has the time to meditate for two hours every day? Most of us don't, so you have to create your own simple reminder. It needs to be something you know you can keep up for the long run; something that will remind you of how amazing you are and that you can handle anything that comes your way. You could keep positive quotes around your house and at your office. You could commit to quiet time once a week for at least half an hour where you self-reflect, pray or do whatever brings you peace. If you can't commit to once a week, then at least try once a month, even if it's only ten minutes.

Step 3-LISTEN TO AUDIO AFFIRMATIONS

You can either record your own affirmations on your phone (which is awesome and powerful) or buy an audio recording of your favorite relaxing affirmations. If possible, try listening to them every morning on your way to work, or maybe once a week on Saturday or Sunday while you run errands.

Step 4-CONNECT WITH LIKE MINDS

Staying in the zone of a better life means being around people who are trying to do the same. Networking doesn't always have to be for business deals. You should network and connect with other women who are also on their path to self-discovery. Whether that means connecting with certain friends more or going to events to meet new people, make sure you create an uplifting environment for yourself. You can visit meetup.com or download their app to help you get started.

Step 5-NURTURE A PLANT

On the path to self-discovery and growth, it's best to have things around you that represent this process.

Buy a small flower or plant that you can water and take care of and watch grow. The seed is you in this journey. Just like the seed needs TLC, so do you. If it helps, you can even give her a little name for fun and make sure you pick a flower that is your favorite color.

Step 6-REWARD YOURSELF

Why should you reward yourself for starting your own path to a deeper relationship with your inner self? The answer is simple. It takes a great amount of courage, will power, and strength to start a journey to one's own self-empowerment. And that is something that definitely deserves rewarding! When you create an annual or bi-annual reward, just knowing that it exists--no matter how big or small--can give you something to look forward to. It can help you stay motivated to stay on your journey. Even if you fall off your journey a million times, then reward yourself just for making an effort to get back on track. When is the last time you went on an adult-only vacation? Go solo, plan a girlfriend's getaway, or go with your significant other, but make sure you do it. If you want it to be extravagant that's fine, but it doesn't have to be.

Step 7-HAVE SHOWER THERAPY

Water has been used to cleanse and give people a sense of renewal since the beginning of time. It can be soothing and represent a fresh start. One suggestion is to make your morning shower a daily healing ritual. You may be in the habit of taking a shower and running through your to-do lists in your head or letting your thoughts run wild about many other topics. If you change that, it may help to shape your day. Get in the shower and be present in that moment. Even if it's a brief shower, try and take those couple minutes to relax your shoulders, take some deep breaths and feel soothed by the warm water. Then imagine the water washing away anything you didn't like that happened the day before or just allow it to represent starting anew.

Step 8-ASK FOR HELP

Unleashing your Goddess Potential is a journey and on this journey you will have a few bumps in the road, fun moments, life lessons and meet interesting people along the way. In order to help you stay consistent on your path, you may sometimes need to ask for help. Asking for help can be a true challenge for some, but you have to remember that no one really successful that you look up to got where they are without asking for help. That help may come in the form of a friend babysitting for free when you don't have the funds so that you can have a date night with self (Principle #1). It may come in the form of some advice from a therapist for help with healing (Principle #6). Regardless, no one gets where they are alone and putting your ego aside to ask for help is one of the most mature, intelligent decisions you can make.

REFLECTING

"Being a mother to twin toddler boys keeps me busy 24/7 and for the first few years I had yearned to have that BFF relationship with God again but I just couldn't seem to find the time. So I decided to make it a routine to say a prayer right after I get the boys in the car. Even though it's not some lengthy meditation session (I love those by the way), it makes me feel good to start out my day this way. Instead of complaining that I didn't have the time, I created something perfect for my lifestyle."

~Ally

"One of the biggest challenges for me was staying consistent with my relationship with the deepest part of me. I would feel the best and handle things so peacefully when I was praying, meditating and journaling on a consistent basis, but when I stopped (and I stopped often) I would feel a little off...just not the same. So now I take a moment when I wake up to affirm how I want the day to start and what I want from it."

~Tara

Ally's Story

My father was never in my life, but an amazing mother and many loving family members balanced it out. I grew up in my grandmother's house in N.W. Washington D.C. I lived there with cousins, aunts, and my mom until I was about thirteen years old. Those years helped shape me. My childhood was filled with fun family cookouts, birthday parties, vacations with my mom, memories of playing in the neighborhood, and even entrepreneurial efforts on my part with several kiddie businesses. I had a mother who always told me I could achieve anything. Every outlandish kiddie business idea was met with positivity and she would help me get the supplies to make it happen. I know now that's a huge part of where my confidence comes from. But things took a turn for me around twelve years old when I came home from a concert with friends to find out that the only father figure I knew (my grandfather) had died from a heart attack. I felt lost, cheated, and devastated with an added layer of shock. I went from a kid who felt totally fulfilled to a lost little girl searching for male attention to fill a hole in my heart. And so started the spiral of bad relationship after bad relationship. My first bad relationship was at thirteen. I thought it was in my twenties but after some deep reflecting I realize I had been on this pattern of dating the same kind of guy ever since I lost my grandfather at twelve. I was thirteen and this boyfriend was fifteen and he was controlling, bossy; always wanted me with him and even threatened to commit suicide if I broke up with him. I ended up dating "him" (same attributes, but different guys) about four times after that throughout high school (with one exception). After high school graduation I followed a boyfriend (the one exception) to Philadelphia to attend college. Enrolling at Temple University started a beautiful journey of self-discovery for me in many ways. I started a women's empowerment magazine, was involved in the campus fashion organization, had many friends, and was a hardworking student. However, my path to self-discovery really began with the tragic and unfortunate death of my seventeen-year-old stepbrother.

One year instead of coming home to Maryland, I stayed in Philadelphia for summer school with one of my best friends. I remember the day like it was yesterday. I came home from class and my friend said, "You need to call your mother right away." When I ended up calling my mother she said, "Your brother shot himself in the head." I paused and just went numb. I was in shock. I drove home to Maryland the next day and those two hours on that highway felt like a lifetime. I got there and after lots of praying and hopeful thoughts my stepbrother passed away a few days later. The day of the funeral I remember sneaking into my mother's off limits living room and lying down on the couch. I knew no one would see me there because no one went in that room. I heard friends and family talking in low voices and could smell the aroma of homemade dishes. I felt a deep heavy grueling sadness... one I had never felt before. It wasn't even the kind I felt when my grandparents died...it was different. This was a young seventeen-year-old and he was supposed to still be alive I thought to myself.

That was the turning point for me. I went from an average college kid who was social and went to parties, to a researching, different church visiting, meditating, and journal-writing young lady. His death made me question life for the first time. Why was I here? What did it all mean? This started a twelve-year spiritual awakening that saved my life. My many experiences that included meeting certain people, having conversations with strangers, journaling, praying, meditating, reflecting, and making many mistakes all helped create who I am today. I am truly thankful for all of it. And during my early twenties I was in a relationship with someone that helped me see the beauty in the Ancient Egyptian culture, lifestyle and life principles, which also contributed to my growth. After that relationship ended I spent the next few years single in New York. I was almost to a point where I felt like giving up on love. I remember telling God that I had so much love to give and I was ready for love. Then I had a change of heart and one day in November of 2010 I decided that I wasn't going to give up on love. I decided that day that I would be open to the process but not obsessed with it. So I signed up for a dating site with an open mind and right after I met two guys from Grenada.

One was in real estate and I can't remember what the other one did. The real estate guy was too busy for a first date and it never went anywhere and I never had real chemistry with the other guy so I just kept it moving but with a positive mindset. Then this amazing thing happened on December 9th, 2010. I was on my way to teach a fashion class to 7th graders in Harlem (I lived in Brooklyn about 45 minutes away). When I got to the top of the subway stairs and saw the train coming something told me to let it pass. Even though I was late, I let that "A" train open and close right in front of me and waited for the next one. I figured if my gut told me to, that it was the right thing to do. I just had this feeling that something would happen that day but I had no idea what. So I got on that first train and then transferred to the express "4" train to head up to Harlem. I was sitting on the train for about 5 stops and it was super-crowded. I was already late and was breaking my neck trying to see the time monitor on the train but a tall woman was blocking it with her head. Then the guy next to me asked me did I need the time. And I looked at him and said, "Yes, thank you," and made some corny joke about me always being late. The rest of the conversation seemed like something from a movie, almost like we knew each other already. I knew my train stop was approaching and he hadn't asked for my number yet. I had never asked for a guy's number before so I needed a sign that he liked me first. I asked him a question and when he replied in a flirty way, that was my sign. I said, "Do you want to stay in touch?" He said "Sure." The next few days and months were spent with long telephone calls, lots of fun dates, and we have literally been inseparable ever since. Now, five years later we are married with three-year-old twin boys and even though our relationship has not always been a walk in the park, I still adore him and feel extremely blessed.

Tara's Story

Growing up in Mississippi, I had my mother, my father, and my three brothers and I later ended up with five more brothers and three sisters. I also had my grandparents and I feel that grandparents are the pavement, which lies beneath the structure on which we are built. Luckily for me I had three grandmothers: my father's mother is my motivation to always push forth because nothing can hold you back, my mother's mother is my intelligence and the need to be as perfect as possible and then there is my mother's biological mother and that is without a doubt where my inadvertent sass and fierce attitude comes from. Between them and my aunts, I embodied all of these different traits that have created who I am today. I have always had these women around with strong personalities. My mom always wanted to please everyone and despite me not being fond of that, it is a trait I definitely got from her. This also made me always want to be good enough to be liked and made me feel like I want to please everyone. As a youth I always sought refuge inside of myself. I always had this knowing and ambition that I could be whatever I wanted in life. Even when I doubted myself I would tell myself, "One day you're going to show them that you can achieve your dreams." So my plan was to be a great actor. That was my huge dream and my desire and I felt that my life would start to happen once I accomplished that goal.

And I started the journey towards achieving that goal when I attended Jackson State University and got a degree in Dramatic Arts. Then I went on to pursue my acting career by enrolling in NY's Actor's Studio Drama School. And in the midst of graduating and getting heavily into the theatre, I met a man and fell in love.

I mean the impact was so strong that it felt like it was meant to be. The love and emotions that developed filled in what was absent and what I felt was missing in the past relationships in my life. I always had this gut feeling in all of my prior relationships that they were all temporary. My two boyfriends in college, while they were fun and both taught me lessons, still felt temporary at the time. I always felt that I was a free bird that may need to stretch her wings or simply fly to new territories at any moment and could not be tied down. That all changed when I met this New York man and fell in love. And for thirteen years we lived together, had some amazing moments, the normal relationship ups and downs, and two beautiful children and it all came to a screeching halt when I found out that he not only cheated on me with someone, but that he had also married her and got her pregnant. The betrayal and whole situation left me feeling like I had a hole in my heart. I was confused, shocked, and deeply saddened.

Although what happened was extremely wrong, I still stepped up to the plate to be mature for my children's sake. Not only was I mature about handling the situation, but I was also protective of the two people who had deeply hurt me. Although I have never defined myself by my relationship status, in this particular situation, I felt like a failure. I'm not sure but I could be in the top twenty-bad breakups of all time, or at least that's how it feels. I spent years down and out about it, feeling alone and betrayed, and being protective of them in the midst of all the hurt and then I had a shimmer of hope, and I started making an effort to find myself so that I could have peace and be happy again. In the midst of my journey towards self-discovery, the father of my two children that I had spent thirteen years of my life with told me he was single again and we briefly explored our feelings for each other and I later discovered I was pregnant. I had a choice and it was to not have the baby or choose to go into the pregnancy being an empowered woman, knowing that I had to be comfortable raising this baby by myself and I chose the latter. Everything happens for a reason and I can honestly say that I am happy and am standing at my conduit of seeing many of my dreams coming true.

Made in the USA
Middletown, DE
26 December 2018